Try Different, Not Harder

Not Harder

KARL G. SCHOEMER

simple ▶ truths®
LEAD TO CHANGE
simpletruths.com

15 Rules for Mastering Change

Editing by: Alice Patenaude

Photo Credits
Cover: front, erhui1979/iStock
Internals: page 1, erhui1979/iStock; page 25, Allies Interactive/Shutterstock, Ohmega1982/Shutterstock; page 33, Ani_Ka/iStock; page 67, phipatbig/Shutterstock; page 99, milo827/Shutterstock; page 107, IhorZigor/Shutterstock; pages 114–115, focal point/Shutterstock; page 123, T-Kot/Shutterstock; page 144, Dooder/Shutterstock; page 152, edel/Shutterstock

Published by Simple Truths, an imprint of Sourcebooks, Inc.
P.O. Box 4410, Naperville, Illinois 60567-4410
(630) 961-3900
Fax: (630) 961-2168
www.sourcebooks.com

Originally published as *The New Reality: How to Make Change Your Competitive Advantage* in 2009 by KGS Inc.

Printed and bound in China.
QL 10 9 8 7 6 5

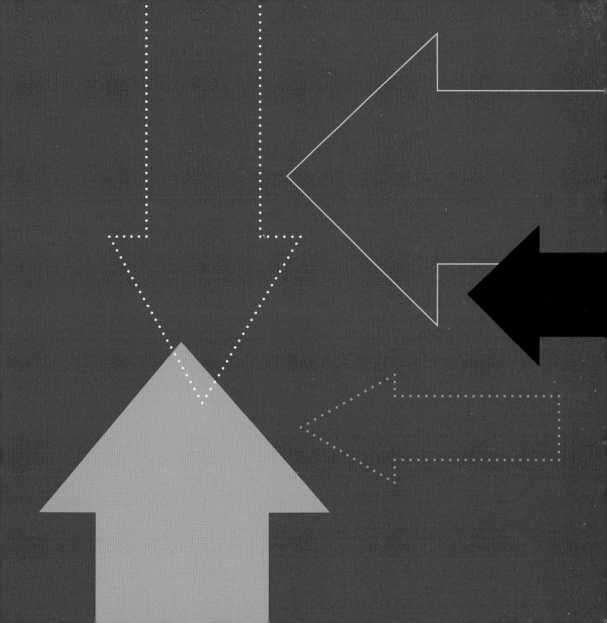

Contents

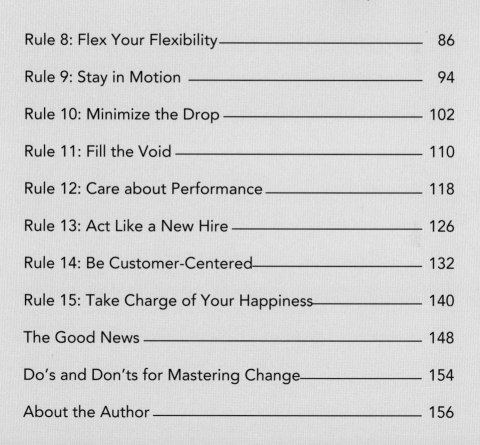

They Are

Things are different. Change is all around us. It's continuous, relentless, and at times overwhelming.

Just where is all this change coming from? Who is driving this?

Higher expectations. Smaller, cheaper, faster, better, safer.

Ridiculous. Unheard of. Unprecedented. What do they think we are? Robots? They are unrealistic. They can't be serious!

Hold on. Just who are "they"?

Who is raising the bar on us? Demanding more, faster, better? You don't know?

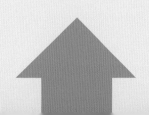

They are us!
We are them!

You can't have it both ways. You can't have it one way as an employee and another as a consumer. You can't expect the latest, greatest, smallest, cheapest, and fastest—and not expect it to have the same impact on what you do.

Regardless of your profession or how you do it, you are them. They are us!

The
NEW

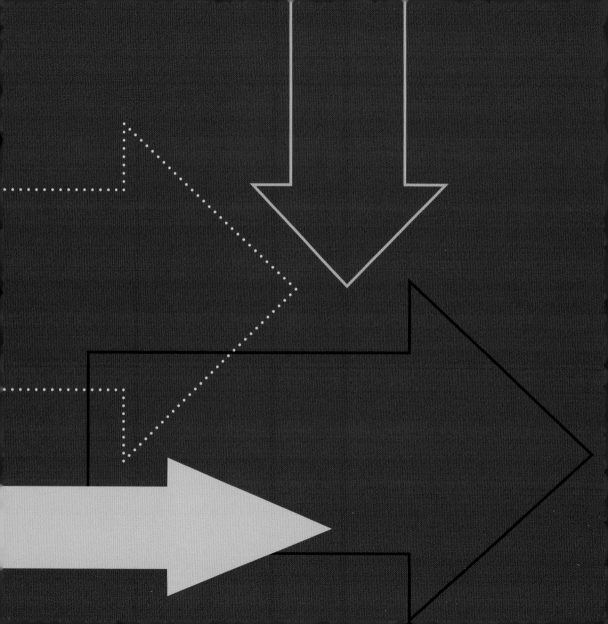

Let's be clear: the opportunities are immense. The information and technology revolution is redefining our work—what it is, how and where it's done, who does it, and how long it takes. We're also reshaping our business organizations—from how they function to what they expect of employees and what employees can expect in return. All of these changes create a tremendously fertile environment for even more change, creating opportunities that are either seized or missed. **It's entirely up to you.**

Sink
or

SWIM

"In business, the competition will bite you
if you keep running;
if you stand still, they will swallow you."

—William S. Knudsen, former chairman, General Motors

Change is here to stay. Those who understand this reality, who accept it and adapt quickly, will emerge profoundly better for it—better in terms of our market value and employability, because we don't squander precious time and energy resisting the inevitable—and certainly better when it comes to our health, happiness, and well-being.

Today, as technology propels change around the globe at warp speed and individuals and organizations struggle to cope, the ability to manage change is as marketable a skill as any we can cultivate, either individually or organizationally. In fact, your goal must be to move yourself through the change process more quickly, easily, and effectively. In today's marketplace, managing change is every organization's single most vital challenge.

Change is impartial. It doesn't care about corporate reputation, size, previous success, or prestige. Nor does it care about personal history, past potential, tenure, or your willingness to try harder. It only rewards those who meet it head-on. No organization can accomplish this unless employees can. Otherwise, the organization is doomed—and, in the short term at least, many employees are doomed as well. According to the John J. Heldrich Center for Workforce Development at Rutgers University, roughly thirty million Americans—or around 20 percent of the workforce—have lost a job during the last five years.

It's clear we must manage change, but managing change is no longer enough. Today's exacting world imposes a new expectation. We must actively seize change and make it work for us. Recognize it as a force in its own right and harness it.

Exploit it. Master it.

All change is about movement, both individually and organizationally. To function at our highest level individually, we must move away from turmoil and toward opportunity, consistently and quickly. Organizations, in turn, must be filled with people doing the same—moving quickly and consistently toward opportunity, the customer, and the marketplace.

With each successive wave of change, stagnant organizations get knocked over and washed away. Others come up for air, coughing and sputtering, but manage to survive. Organizations that excel, on the other hand, maintain the momentum that enables them to catch each new wave. And when they're not catching waves, they're making them. They can do this only if they are filled with people working in unison, traveling the competitive currents like a school of fish, moving individually, yet as one, toward opportunity and away from danger.

Slow-moving fish are a feast waiting to happen, bait for the taking. The last to move will perish. In the pages ahead are some swimming lessons. Read them, learn them, practice them—and avoid being the last fish.

"In today's rapidly changing world,
    if you always do what you've always done,

you'll get less than you've always gotten.
Changing technology, decreasing margins,
and increasing competition will see to that."

—Karl G. Schoemer, founder and president, VisionQuest

Operating

This book offers you guidelines and tools that can help you seize change and master it.

Read it. Then go back and read it again. Take some time—an afternoon, a week, a month—whatever time you need for the ideas to sink in.

These ideas address global themes that should be familiar to anyone immersed in today's dramatically changing workplace. They are designed to jump-start your thinking and prod you to action.

However, when it comes to your job, you are the expert. You know what works and what doesn't, what you can do and what you can't, what makes sense and what doesn't. Ultimately, only you know what actions to take and when.

Each of the fifteen rules explored in these pages is accompanied by suggestions to improve your performance and change your personal competitive advantage. The actions you take may spell the difference between success and failure in a radically changing world.

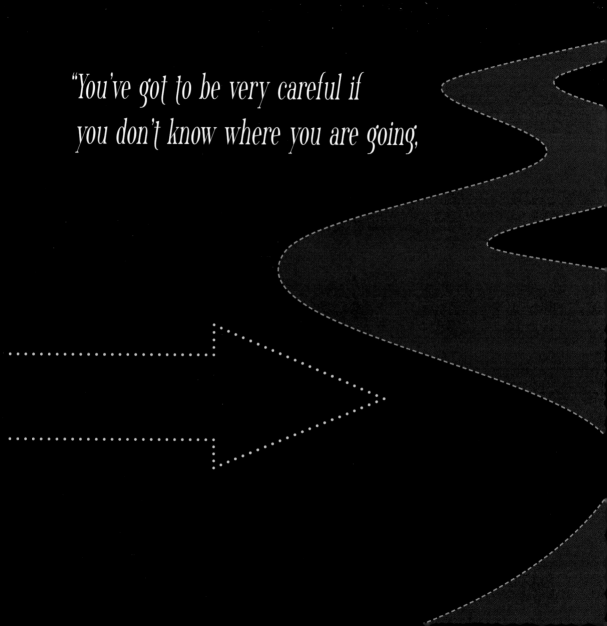

"You've got to be very careful if
you don't know where you are going,

because you might not get there."

—Lawrence Peter "Yogi" Berra,
former New York Yankees catcher and coach

REWRITE the

Contract

"It is the nature of man as he grows older to protest against change, particularly change for the better."

—John Steinbeck, author

"I will come in every day and do what you want, when you want it, how you want it. I'll toe the line. I won't rock the boat. I won't take risks. In return, you will give me a job for the rest of my life."

This unwritten contract between employers and employees is extinct. The old corporate ethic rewarded longevity and tenure and implied the promise of stability. Compliant, conforming employees survived—and, in fact, many thrived. These were the people who were recognized, rewarded, and promoted.

This has changed.
It's gone!

We can no longer expect loyal compliance to be rewarded with cradle-to-grave job security.

Organizations can't compete based on the number of people who simply show up. Attendance is not a competitive advantage. Nowadays, it's all about performance. Outcome trumps effort. This fundamental change has unsettled those of us who grew up in the old environment honoring the old contract. Many of us feel confused or betrayed.

Such feelings are understandable, but they are debilitating burdens in today's business culture. Cling to the belief that the old contract still applies, or should apply, and each successive change places you at greater risk. Remain rooted to outworn ideology, and you diminish in value daily.

> "They're asking me to do things today that would have gotten me fired five years ago."

The rules are different now. The behaviors that, for years, got people promoted can now result in being left behind. Likewise, the independent decisions that, in the past, led to punitive actions are coveted and sought after today. The desire for unquestioning compliance has been replaced with the need for creative discontent.

"Come, my friends,
'Tis not too late to seek a new

—Alfred, Lord Tenn

er world."

yson, poet

O DO

Accept that the old contract is history. Bring value, and bring it daily. Be a creative, flexible leader. Think for yourself. Seek solutions, not problems. Challenge the status quo. Rock the boat. Be the person you would want on your staff if you owned the company. Draw a bright line of distinction between the old environment and the new.

Stalk the

TRUTH

"Judge a man by his questions rather than by his answers."

—Voltaire, philosopher

"Just tell me the answer. If I just knew the answer, everything would be okay."

It is no longer acceptable to expect answers simply to be handed to you. Need an answer? Go get it. You've already asked? Ask again. Or ask someone else. Be aware, though, that the nature of answers has changed.

For one thing, if you get an answer you don't like, it doesn't mean your question wasn't answered. Nor does it mean that nobody communicates with you.

Answers have become far more perishable. The breakneck pace of technology has made truth a moving target. What was true two weeks ago may no longer be true today. That doesn't mean what was said two weeks ago was a lie, nor does it make the speaker untrustworthy.

Another consequence of spiraling change is that "I don't know" has become perfectly valid. However, ambiguity tends to make us uncomfortable, so "I don't know" is a tough answer to give and receive. But it's a response we must learn to accept. Any other answer might be inaccurate or even irresponsible.

In the old environment, we used to pay managers to have all the answers. In the new environment, it's impossible for anyone to have all the answers. Things are moving too fast. If you're trying to provide or get all the answers, you're hurting yourself. It's far better to say or hear "I don't know" than to circulate half-truths or gossip. It's better to say "I don't know—I'll try to find out." It's even better—in these times of empowerment, contribution, and participation—to say "What do you think?"

No one has all the answers.

Answers are different now.

Accept these two truths, and the cloud of ambiguity will begin to dissipate.

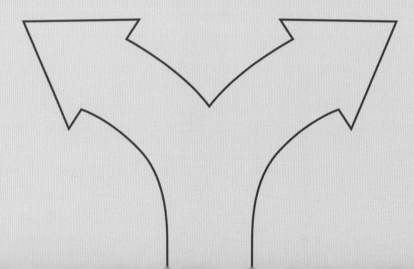

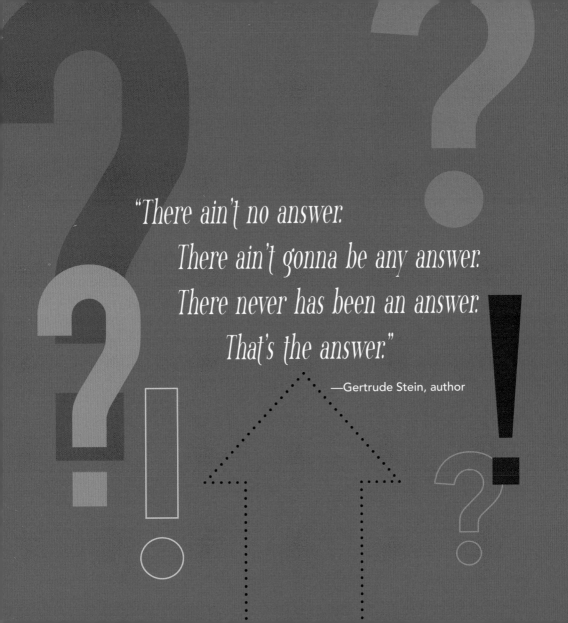

"There ain't no answer.
There ain't gonna be any answer.
There never has been an answer.
That's the answer."

—Gertrude Stein, author

WHAT
TO DO

Go get the answers. If your boss can't give them to you, ask your boss's boss or someone else in the organization. Expect that those answers will change—soon. Choose your answer battles carefully, but choose them and wage them; the bigger risk is to do nothing. Formulate good answers on your own using the best information available, but never shy away from saying "I don't know." Accept it as a valid statement, whether you're on the giving or receiving end.

Try
DIFFERENT,

Not Harder

"*The only sense that is common in the long run, is the sense of change—and we all instinctively avoid it.*"

—E. B. White, author

"I can't work any harder. I'm already working harder than I ever have."

This common complaint during times of change is a red flag. No reorganization, reengineering, or right sizing sets an objective to have people work harder or longer. The goal is not to have fewer people do the same amount of work but to have fewer people figure out which part of the work is most important to the customer and do that.

Underlying the change, though, is a marketplace mandate for greater efficiency, productivity, and levels of service. So while you need not necessarily work harder, you definitely must work differently.

The problem is that our competence and confidence lies in the old tools and methods. We are more comfortable redoubling our efforts than changing them.

"The way we've been doing it has always been good enough, so more of the same should be better."

Just when we should be letting go of the old, the ambiguity and uncertainty of change make us grip it even more tightly. Instead of giving the wheelbarrow a try, we feverishly attempt to move rocks more quickly by hand.

"How can my work suddenly be unacceptable? I'm doing exactly what I've always done, exactly how I've always done it."

Productivity is now gauged not only by the end result, but also by the processes and tools you use and your willingness to change those processes and tools. If you're still doing your job the way you always have by gritting your teeth, working longer and harder, and digging in your heels against change, every day puts you farther behind. In fact, if you simply do more of what you have always done, you'll get less than you ever have.

What worked yesterday won't necessarily work today. Good vaccines become ineffective against adaptive viruses. Even the best major league pitchers eventually give up a hit if they don't constantly revise their strategies. The tendency to do more of what made you successful is natural, but what made you successful may not *keep* you successful.

"If the only tool you have is a hammer, you tend to see every problem as a nail."

—Abraham Maslow, psychologist

WHAT TO DO

Fight your natural resistance to change. Figure out what needs to be done. Find out what no longer needs to be done, then stop doing it. Separate the wheat from the chaff and invest your time and energy in the wheat. Don't do more with less; do more by doing it differently. Work smarter. Perpetually adjust, refine, innovate, adapt.

Separate
Loyalty

from
PERFORMANCE

"Too many people are thinking of security instead of opportunity. They seem more afraid of life than death."

—James F. Byrnes, politician

"We used to be such a family around here. Now they obviously don't care about us. You can't even trust anyone anymore."

Trust and loyalty are seductive concepts. We readily expect them, grudgingly bestow them, and mistakenly equate them with job security. "As long as my company provides job security," the thinking goes, "I consider it trustworthy and loyal—deserving of my trust and loyalty in return."

But in an age of vanishing job security, employee loyalty is diminishing as well.

"I'll just do my job and nothing more. I'll put my time in and then leave. They won't get anything extra from me."

What is employee loyalty? Going above and beyond? Putting in extra time? Performing better than expected? Regardless of how you exhibit loyalty, when you withdraw it out of resentment, who is at risk? If you cloak yourself in a cloud of distrust because you no longer have job security and you're angry about it, who gets hurt?

Most companies would like to provide some sense of job security, but no organization can be more loyal than the marketplace allows. Today's marketplace is intense, tough, and unforgiving. The competition is worldwide and world-class. What would become of an NBA or NFL team that made its roster decisions based on loyalty or sentiment? Or an army command that made tactical decisions based on what its troops would prefer? Loyalty has its place, but if it strips the company of its ability to compete, it's dangerous. A lean, productive, well-managed organization can employ more people than a bankrupt one can.

But even though organizations can no longer guarantee job security, that doesn't mean they are not loyal. The loyalty lies in trying to make the company as successful as possible. Doing that creates and keeps jobs.

Let's separate this loyalty discussion from performance, once and for all. In the New Reality, the organization trades performance for money. You perform, the company pays you. Period. The better you perform, the more they pay you. The longer you perform, the longer they pay you.

Be loyal to your performance, and it will be loyal to you.

Performance

Support

Quality

Goals

"*Only foolish people are completely secure.*"

—John Kenneth Galbraith, economist

Satisfaction

WHAT
TO DO

Separate loyalty from performance, and differentiate yourself through your performance. Realize that your employer isn't your family. Invest your loyalty in yourself, your skills, and your future. Increase your employability in the world at large by expanding your opportunities inside your organization. Volunteer for every new assignment that comes along. Enroll in every educational program that's offered. Cross-train for as many jobs as possible. Find a mentor. Focus on learning.

EMBRACE

Openness

"*Anybody who isn't confused isn't well informed.*"

—Anonymous

"I wish they would make up their minds. Every week I hear something different."

Communication is the handmaiden of change. Without constant, consistent communication, change creates division, confusion, and chaos. In football, the result is called a broken play. In business, it's called inefficiency, mismanagement, or a fourth-quarter loss.

Nothing is set in stone, or even sand. The best-laid plan, structure, process, or system will change—probably soon. This accelerated pace has complicated communication in the workplace. Here's a typical scenario. You get information about a change that needs to be communicated, so you convey it to colleagues. But within weeks or even days, the information is no longer accurate. The result? Your colleagues' trust and confidence in you decrease.

But, quick study that you are, the next time you get some information, you take a different tack. Not wanting to frustrate people by inadvertently leading them astray, you hold on to the information while you check out its accuracy. Meanwhile, your colleagues get it from another source. The result? Their trust and confidence in you decrease.

So, the next time you get some information, you do…what?

What you must do is share everything you know, but always attach a strong tagline. In the past, "subject to change" was a sufficient disclaimer. Not anymore. Today, it's impossible to overemphasize the likelihood of change: "This will change. I don't know how. I don't know when. But it will change." Remember to be forthright about what you don't know. If you don't know, say "I don't know."

In the Old Reality, trustworthiness was defined according to your answer's shelf life. The longer it stayed the way you said it was going to be, the more they could believe you, the more they could trust you! But you can't use the same definition of trustworthiness in the New Reality.

"I know I said last Monday that was the way we were going to do it. I know this Monday I said this was the way we were going to do it. Even though the two are different doesn't mean you can't trust me or believe me. With what we knew last week, we were going to do it that way. With what we know this week, we are going to do it this way. The change has nothing to do with whether you can trust or believe me."

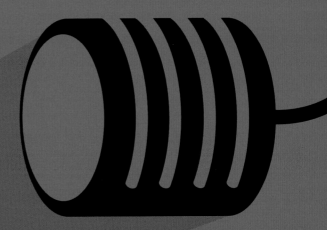

"The single biggest problem
in communication
is the illusion that
it has taken place."

—George Bernard Shaw, playwright

WHAT
TO DO

Promise change. Say "for now" as often as possible. Stop defining believability by how long information is valid. Share everything, good or bad. Be honest. Don't hold on to information. Move it as fast as you get it. Instead of conveying large blocks of information infrequently, give short bursts continuously. Clearly say, hear, and accept "this will change."

Deliver QUICKER

Quality

"'Perfect' is the enemy of 'good enough.'"

—Meg Whitman, chief executive officer, Hewlett Packard

"Slow down and do it right the first time.
Eliminate deviations."

Emphasis on quality proved a saving grace for many companies in the 1980s. Unfortunately, the shift toward total quality management ran headlong into the exponentially accelerating pace of change. Total quality is now the price of admission. Merely meeting customer expectations puts us behind competitors who are exceeding those expectations.

The marketplace has added time as a critical component of quality. Quality isn't quality unless it's timely. The principle isn't new, but our concept of timeliness is. Timeliness today requires speed that only recently was unfathomable. Achieving that speed calls for constantly upgrading our processes and tools. No upgrade, no timeliness. No timeliness, no quality.

As crucial as quality is, if we fail to deliver the product or service when the customer needs it, even exquisite quality loses its value. More players enter the game daily. Technology continues to shrink the world and intensify competition. As a result, customers can and do demand unprecedented speed. Timeliness is the customer's call—not yours, not your boss's, not the CEO's.

The time we have to get it right is no longer unlimited. Now, we must not only get it right the first time, but we also must do it faster and better than ever. Impossible? That's a tempting response, but it's demonstrably wrong. We either accept this challenge or put our company at a severe competitive disadvantage. If we don't do it, somebody else will. In fact, somebody else is already doing it.

Quality is everybody's job. So is quickly aligning with the customer. Here's the important part: they are not mutually exclusive. It's not one or the other; it's both! Move quickly to align with the marketplace, and continuously improve the quality of what you deliver. Do this—and you are delivering "quicker quality."

"The only way to discover
the limits of the possible is to go
beyond them into the impossible."

—Arthur C. Clarke, author

WHAT
TO DO

Step on the gas. Don't just improve the process; look critically to see if the process is even necessary anymore. Try it out. See if it works. Don't study it to death. Forget perfect: you need to be fast and good enough. Trust your intuition. Be crystal clear on the customer's definition of quality; ask, then ask again. Critique every process with timeliness in mind. Inject urgency at every turn. When measuring quality, always include speed.

MOVE
Your

Mastery

"Hindsight is much more accurate than foresight, but not as valuable."

—Dwight D. Eisenhower, U.S. president

"Just slow this thing down and let me get as good at this as I was at that."

We used to be able to master things—the system, the technology, the structure. Not anymore. At least, not like before.

Today, we need to shift our focus from mastering the change to *mastering change*.

Any system, process, or technology is temporary. This isn't a revelation. Heraclitus, who said, "There is nothing permanent except change," was on to it more than 2,450 years ago. Technologies and systems have become so temporary that the journey from one to the next is the predominant state. This is where we must exercise mastery over the journey—

over getting from here to there...and there...and there. Transition is not a temporary phase to get through; it's the element we live in now. It's the oxygen that sustains the whole system.

Today, mastery is measured by how well we foresee and adapt, how quickly we move, how fast we can let go of the old and grab hold of the new. To achieve it, we must violate that screaming instinct to resist all things new and different.

Your ability and willingness to adapt, to move, to change— quickly and effectively—are as marketable as any skill you possess. The value you bring to the organization comes as much from your ability to get from here to there as any other competency.

Master the movement. Master the transition. Master the white space between here   and   there.

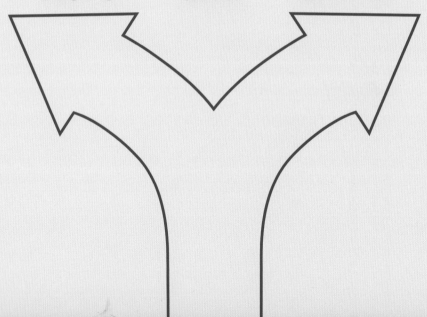

"If we watch ourselves honestly,
we shall often find that we have
begun to argue against a new idea
even before it has been
completely stated."

—Wilfred Trotter, neurosurgeon and social psychologist

WHAT
TO DO

Master the process. Become better at change than everyone you know. Ask questions. Speed up. Look for the opportunity to practice your change management skills. Better yet, create opportunities to practice. Change the criteria: don't measure success by getting through it; measure success by getting here…there…everywhere. Reward masters of change. Continually improve the process of change. Be the first to try.

Flex Your

FLEXIBILITY

"It's what you learn after you know it all that counts."

—John Wooden, Hall of Fame basketball coach

"Just give me some time to get used to the idea. I'll warm up to this in a month or so."

In the old environment, there was time to adjust. People had the chance to get comfortable, to work through their resistance to any changes occurring around them.

Now, as the global marketplace grows more complex daily, competition can and does come from any quarter. The luxury of time to adjust is gone, and failure can descend more quickly than ever.

How long do you have to work through your resistance? Unfortunately, you don't get to decide. Neither does your boss or your organization. The limits are set by the marketplace, by your customers.

"I just don't like the new system. What was wrong with the old way?"

Your willingness to adapt quickly becomes a competitive advantage—individually and organizationally. Similarly, your unwillingness or inability to quickly adapt becomes a huge competitive disadvantage—for you and for your organization.

Look around. There are people in your organization, in your department, maybe even in the same job, who are thriving on all this change. If they have adjusted and you haven't, who is at risk? Who is vulnerable? Who is unhappy? Embrace change or it will hunt you down—exposing your rigidity and diminishing your value.

How can you increase your flexibility? Two words: **let go.** That's right. Let go. Let go of the past, the old process, the old thinking, the old approach or method. Let go of your perception of the "good old days." Let go of old work habits and expectations.

Do this—
and you will begin to flex your flexibility.

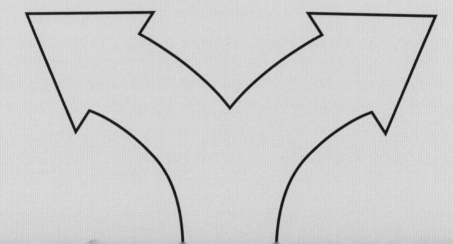

"The past always looks better than it was.
It's only pleasant because it isn't here."

—Finley Peter Dunne, humorist

WHAT
TO DO

Bring a sense of adventure to work each day. Make your reputation on how quickly you adapt. Question your resistance. Don't hold on to the old way. Don't waste precious energy digging in. Be the first to try. Fix it on the fly.

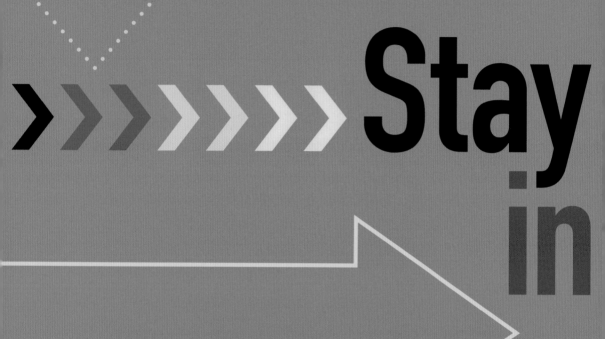

Stay in

MOTION

"How dull it is to pause, to make an end, to rust unburnished, not to shine in use!"

—Alfred, Lord Tennyson, poet

"Just tell me the effective date, the roll-out date. Once we get past that, everything will be okay; things will get back to normal."

Change is a process, not an event. Characterizing it as an event implies there is a start and a stop. There is no beginning or end to change. It is constant and will continue to be.

"If I hold my breath until this thing passes, until it goes away, until it runs its course, I'll be okay. I've seen these 'programs of the month' come and go."

Back to normal? This is normal. Any reference to change as temporary or isolated gives people a reason to wait for it to pass and implies a false sense of reality. It will not pass. It will not blow over.

"Just give me a minute. One thing at a time. I'll be ready for that next week."

A lot of people are holding their breath, waiting to see. How long can you wait? How long can you go without breathing? Every minute you wait puts you farther behind the competition—individually and organizationally. Change won't go away. In fact, it will go even faster.

In the Old Reality, we were able to finish—the project, the process, the upgrade. Finish learning the new system. Finish the change.

Not anymore. The language of delay and deferral that was once so common in the workplace has become unacceptable. The pace of modern business requires us to start the new before finishing the old. The satisfaction of closure has been replaced by the satisfaction of adaptability, by the instantaneous ability to change.

"*If you don't drive your business,*
you will be driven out of business."

—B. C. Forbes, founder, *Forbes* magazine

WHAT
TO DO

Stop waiting. Try. Adapt. Stop holding your breath. Instead, breathe in the air of "What if? Why not? Let's try it. Let's go." Be proactive. Improve it. Change it. Predict the next change. Suggest the next change. Already be there when everyone else catches up. Give up trying to complete everything. Adopt versatility. Let go of your attachment to closure. Don't invest yourself in finishing a project that, due to changes, may not need to be finished. Be willing and able to not only change horses midstream, but also to change streams.

MINIMIZE

the Drop

"The handwriting on the wall may be a forgery."

—Ralph Hodgson, poet

"I know the organization is expecting more of me. They need me to change, so I will. I will just do more of the old. There, I changed!"

All major changes carry with them a temporary drop in productivity. Some will dispute this, but only if they're measuring output without regard to input. Look at the overtime, documented or not, that people put in during times of change. Look at the work people take home. Look at the stress, the anxiety, the frustration. If, in the wake of change, productivity doesn't dip, it's only because people are working harder to compensate for the temporary drop in efficiency.

"It didn't work! We need to go back, forward, up, down, sideways."

You have to get through this drop in productivity as quickly as possible—if for no other reason than to prepare for the next change—because there will be a next change. Eventually, productivity will rebound. It should even exceed old levels. After all, that's why the organization made the change in the first place. But the transition time absolutely must be kept to a minimum. This wasn't as crucial before as it is now. We had time to get comfortable, to assimilate the changes one by one. That's no longer the case. Today, it can mean the difference between success and failure or the life or death of an organization.

It's imperative to equip yourself with the skills necessary to manage through the transition quickly. Otherwise, a false shadow of failure can be cast on the change itself.

Like the prospector who abandons a claim within a single ax swing of striking ore, an organization might mistakenly abandon a good change—a change that was right all along.

"Life is like riding a bicycle.
You don't fall off unless you stop pedaling."

—Claude Pepper, U.S. politician

WHAT
TO DO

Anticipate the productivity drop and recognize it when it arrives. Be mindful that the speed of the transition is critical. Overcome your discomfort and awkwardness as fast as possible through learning and practice. Reread the plan. Find a mentor. Focus on the gains.

FILL the

VOID →

"Iron rusts from disuse;
water loses its purity from stagnation...
even so does inaction sap the vigors of the mind."

—Leonardo da Vinci, painter and scientist

"How could I be harming this organization by continuing to do what I've always done—what I have been paid, rewarded, and promoted to do? As soon as they make up their minds, I'll gladly go along. In the meantime…"

Change creates voids—in communication, leadership, information, authority, decision making, risk taking, innovation…

Inevitably, many people respond by not responding, by waiting passively for the voids to be filled before they move forward.

"Someone needs to fix this. I can't do anything because no one told me, directed me, explained it to me, or approved me."

Those who fill the void stand out. They are held up as heroes. They make their customers happy. They make their boss's job easier. They increase effectiveness and make themselves more valuable. And, by the way—they are usually more satisfied, less stressed and frustrated, and generally happier.

It is the waiting that is silently killing off good organizations every day. Riding the winds of all radical change is a classic paradox. Safe is dangerous. Holding steady creates more turmoil. Waiting for your path to be free of voids actually creates more of them. Those who wait think they are doing no harm.

"I'm just doing my job, the way you taught me to, pay me to, told me to. As soon as you tell me what to do differently—exactly and specifically—I will."

Those who passively wait are slowly but surely jeopardizing the future of their organization and, therefore, their own jobs.

"It is not enough to be industrious; so are the ants. What are you industrious about?"

—Henry David Thoreau, author

WHAT TO DO

Step up. Volunteer. Challenge the status quo. Spot the voids before anyone else. Call attention to them, and get them filled. Give others detailed directions on how to fill them. Encourage them. Coach them. Identify those who are filling the voids—then recognize, reward, and promote them.

CARE
about

PERFORMANCE

"We are not endeavoring to get ahead of others,
but to surpass ourselves."

—Hugh B. Brown, prominent leader,
the Church of Jesus Christ of Latter-day Saints

"What will they give me? What am I owed? What can I get? Raises every year, promotions every two years, job security, more vacation time, my birthday off?"

Somehow things got turned upside down. Obligations and responsibilities shifted from those who work for the organization to the organization itself. Entitlements and benefits took center stage. The organization's success and prestige were measured in no small part by how much it "cared" about its people—how much it gave them, how fat the benefits, perks, and extras were.

Organizations that didn't provide these things were antiquated, considered cold and uncaring. Then came the restructurings, followed by layoffs, followed by reorganizations, followed by layoffs, followed by reengineering, followed by...well, you get the idea.

Amid all this tumult, the outcry about heartless, callous organizations became even louder.

"They don't care about people any longer. It's all about the bottom line. Corporate greed."

Hold it!

The mistake was not in rescinding guaranteed employment, raises, and promotions. It was in implying that employees were automatically entitled to them in the first place. Entitlement is a slippery slope. What was "extra" this year is expected the next.

Institutional paternalism creates a vicious cycle of growing expectations and subsequent disappointments. Managers who care more about the individual than the organization do them both a disservice. In today's marketplace, no company can withstand that burden over time.

Let's get back to the very foundation of our market-driven economy—the fabric of our society and the reason there are *any* jobs. Performance counts! It's the only thing that counts. Without it, everything else is meaningless or nonexistent. Care about performance—yours, that of others, and the organization's. If we all do this, we have our best shot at success.

"Frankly, I don't believe people think of their office as a workplace anyway. I think they think of it as a stationery store with Danish. You want to get your pastry, your envelopes, your supplies, your toilet paper, six cups of coffee, and you go home."

—Jerry Seinfeld, comedian

WHAT
TO DO

Care more about your performance than what your employer can do for you. Give up the entitlement mentality. Expect more from yourself. Build your own employment security. Make your performance expectations clear to others. Be sure you know what others expect from you. Create your own benefits.

ACT
Like a

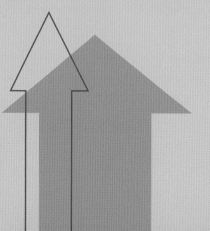

NEW Hire

"Only a mediocre person is always at his best."

—W. Somerset Maugham, author

"I can't do that! How much more are they going to ask of me? I don't need this anymore..."

Who most often asks "Why do we do it this way?" Who usually has a wealth of new ideas to help improve a process? Who is usually the most willing to do whatever it takes? Who is eager to learn, to try new things? Who is ready and willing to start with a clean slate?

In each case, the answer is—a new hire. Where do new hires come from? Old jobs. Ironically, the people so willing to do whatever it takes in a new job are often the same ones who were negative and resistant in the old job.

In fact, many of them left the old job because they thought they couldn't or didn't want to do what was being asked of them. Often, the changes they now regard as fresh and innovative at their new place of employment are the exact same changes that were "impossible" at the old place.

The difference between "I can't do it" and "I'll do whatever it takes" need not involve a change of address. All it takes is a change of perspective. It makes no sense to resist change now, only to welcome it elsewhere later.

"Nothing great was ever achieved without enthusiasm."

—Ralph Waldo Emerson, philosopher and author

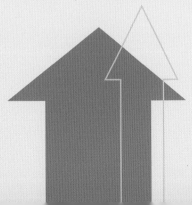

WHAT TO DO

Treat each day like a new job. Try to bring a fresh perspective. Make a habit of asking why. Refuse to accept "because we've always done it that way." Skip the resistance. Clean the slate. Be the employee you would want to hire.

Be
Customer-

CENTERED

"I don't have any contact with the customer. All my customers are internal. I'm in a staff, administrative, support role. I don't talk to the customer, see the customer, or interact with the customer. That's a sales job. My job has nothing to do with the customer."

In the New Reality, those sentiments couldn't be more wrong. Everything everybody does is—or should be—for the customer. They are our reason for being employed. Take away customers, and the need for your job vanishes.

Every person in the organization needs to clearly understand three things when it comes to customers: who they are, what they want, and how each job connects to giving them what they want.

Here are some other examples of customer disconnects:

> "This is a big company. We are in research and development. This is a nonprofit. Patients aren't customers. All I do is assembly. This is a manufacturing site. Information technology is internal. I've never even talked to a customer!"

Wrong again. Every organization, company, group, association, agency, or entity has customers. There is ultimately someone we are doing the job for. Every employee should know who that is and what they expect—regardless of the job, role, purpose, or size of the organization. Today's employers need to be built on serving the customer. They need to be turned sideways so everyone can clearly see the customer.

"If it weren't for those pesky customers, my job would be easy. I could get my work done if I wasn't being constantly interrupted by customers. If the phone would just stop ringing, I'd be a lot more productive. I'm just not in the mood to deal with them. They are unrealistic in their expectations."

Customers are who they are. They want what they want. If you don't give it to them, somebody else will. It's an old adage, but never truer than today. Customers sign our paychecks. We work for them. They are our boss. They call the shots. If not for them, there would be no us.

In the New Reality, every employee needs to understand just how important customers are—and act accordingly. We also need to understand that customer expectations are a moving target. They change, shift, and grow. The only way to move with them is to be agile, mobile, and adaptive—in short, to make change a part of your competitive advantage.

"There is only one boss.
        The customer.
And he can fire everybody in the company
        from the chairman on down,
        simply by spending his money somewhere else."

—Sam Walton, founder, Wal-Mart Stores, Inc.

WHAT TO DO

Introduce yourself to your customers. Know your customers and your customer's customers. Understand how your job adds value for customers. Understand your customers' expectations. Strive to exceed those expectations daily. Thank your customers and delight them.

Take CHARGE
of Your

Happiness

"Happiness is nothing more than good health and a bad memory."

—Albert Schweitzer, physician and philosopher

"It's not the way it used to be. It used to be better in the old days. I don't like it around here anywhere near as well as I once did. It's not fair."

Things are definitely different today—faster, more complex, full of change. We have higher expectations, less security, less stability, and less time for chitchat.

Definitely different.

Unfortunately, many people equate "different" with "bad." "Not the same" means "worse." The old days were always better than now. Back in the day, organizations cared about people, and people cared back. Because of all this change, we have lost the human touch. People aren't happy anymore. It's just a cold, callous job.

Wait a minute.

There are two important points to consider when talking about happiness. First, you will never make everybody happy! Stop trying. Give it up. Forget about it. Whether you change or don't, change a lot or a little, change fast or slow, you won't make everybody happy. As you well know, for some, nothing you do will make them happy.

The second and most important point is that happiness is a choice! Your morale and satisfaction are also personal choices.

Take charge of your own happiness. It's a key part of surviving and thriving in the New Reality.

"The greatest part of our happiness depends on our dispositions, not our circumstances."

—Martha Washington, First Lady

WHAT
TO DO

Stop grumbling. Accept this reality. Let go of the past. Start fresh. Look for opportunity. Find solutions. Move forward. Reevaluate priorities. Take care of yourself. Make your own happiness.

The
GOOD

News

Opportunities today are so widespread that the challenge has become sorting through them.

The willingness to try new approaches is a behavior prized by front-runners. Dynamic organizations seek agents of change, those who can create centers of influence capable of moving the process along. Today, people who can master change are seen as heroes. They are recognized and rewarded. Those who can drive change and take the knocks develop a thick skin of conviction—a highly regarded asset.

Change is not without risk, but most people don't realize the real risk is in waiting.

The good news: once you make the decision to let go, to move forward, to make change your competitive advantage, you instantaneously propel yourself past the masses. You immediately become someone with whom organizations want to consult and partner.

The game has changed with new rules, new players, and a New Reality. And it will continue to change. Almost everyone is just as much in the dark as you are about what the next version of the game will be.

So the playing field is level—for an instant. Help define the new rules, and you not only gain an advantage, but you also reduce your own uncertainty.

The astonishing pace of change today has created a business environment verging on controlled chaos. Organizations are responding to this upheaval by giving more people greater opportunities to take control.

So, figure out what you can control— what piece, what aspect, what detail— and get busy controlling it.

Your experience is valuable. It's gotten you where you are now.

Experience in and of itself is no longer good enough unless it's sheathed in the proper outlook. Believe in yourself. Make your most important skill that of developing new skills. Successful people do what unsuccessful people don't like to do.

Make change your personal competitive advantage, and write your own ticket instead of waiting for someone else to punch it. It can be done. Make your own good news.

Stay true to these lessons, and you too can master change!

DO'S AND ■ ■■■■■ FOR

DO act.
DO align yourself with customers.
DO try.
DO be resilient.
DO question.
DO look ahead.
DO move quickly.
DO commit to the new.
DO challenge the status quo.
DO plan.
DO analyze.
DO bring energy.
DO give your all.
DO celebrate success.
DO step up.
DO say "for now."
DO update your skills.
DO take risks.
DO add value.
DO be flexible.
DO innovate.
DO contribute.

MASTERING CHANGE

wait to act.
malign your customers.
try just once.
be resistant.
attack.
focus behind.
drag your feet.
be committed to the old.
cling to the status quo.
plan indefinitely.
overanalyze.
misdirect energy.
give up.
celebrate others' failures.
step aside.
say "forever."
think your current skills are good enough.
fear failure.
value the past.
be inflexible.
instigate.
contribute to resistance.

About the
the

AUTHOR

Karl G. Schoemer is founder and president of VisionQuest, which specializes in helping organizations integrate change. Since 1990, Karl has shared his expertise on five continents with clients such as AT&T, IBM, JPMorgan Chase, Procter & Gamble, Ford Motor Company, the National Security Agency, Intel, Johnson & Johnson, the Army Tank Command, and hundreds of other organizations.

Would you like to learn more?

Choose from a variety of services and approaches, including:

➜ Keynote addresses

➜ Workshops

➜ Individual coaching

➜ Training retreat facilitation

➜ Comprehensive communication programs

➜ Organization-wide interventions

FOR DETAILS, CALL OR WRITE:

VisionQuest

39 Timber Lane

Brownsburg, IN 46112

Phone: (317) 858-1944; (800) 883-7292

Fax: (317) 858-1945

Karl.Schoemer@vqsolutions.com

www.vqsolutions.com

How to Make Change Your Competitive Advantage